D1549410

THE INDIAN COOKBOOK

MRIDULA BALJEKAR

TIGER BOOKS INTERNATIONAL
LONDON

INTRODUCTION

The vastness of the Indian subcontinent, together with its great regional diversity, is one of the main factors that give the nation's cuisine its unique standing in the culinary world. Amongst other things, however, Indian food reflects the colourful and varied life of its people – their history, culture and religion.

From Afghanistan and the Middle East came the Mughals, a regal race of Muslims, bringing with them exotic spices and dried fruit and nuts, which they combined with milk and cream to concoct the rich 'Mughlai' dishes that are characteristic of northern India. The Kashmiris, too, made a notable contribution with their use of saffron and other rare spices, giving Indian recipes, especially sweets and puddings, a festive touch. Persian, Greek, Roman, Mongol, Portuguese and British are among the many other cultures that have both given to and learned from the cookery of India – and the process continues.

Today, Indian cuisine enjoys unprecedented popularity throughout the Western world. Most people's experience of it, however, has been limited to the dishes offered by restaurants. Excellent though this food often is, there is much pleasure and variety to be gained from preparing Indian meals at home. Spices are nowadays readily available in Indian speciality stores as well as supermarkets, and even the more exotic ingredients can be found without too much trouble, and by adjusting quantities to suit your taste, a wide variety of flavours can be created.

Appetising in aroma and tempting to the palate, Indian cooking is also healthy. The medicinal properties of ingredients such as cloves, garlic, onions and various spices are widely accepted, and their everyday use in Indian cuisine means that the tempting dishes in this book will delight your tastebuds and care for your body.

3135
This edition published in 1992 by Tiger Books International PLC, London
© 1992 Coombe Books
Printed and bound in Singapore
All rights reserved
ISBN 1-85501-229-4

CHICKEN TIKKA

Chicken Tikka is one of the most popular chicken dishes cooked in the Tandoor, the Indian clay oven. This recipe is adapted to cook the chicken in the conventional oven at a high temperature.

SERVES 4

450g/1lb boneless, skinned chicken breast
1 tsp salt
Juice of ½ a lemon
½ tsp tandoori colour or a few drops of
    red food colouring mixed with
    1 tbsp tomato purée
2 cloves garlic, peeled and coarsely
    chopped
½-inch cube of root ginger, peeled and
    coarsely chopped
2 tsps ground coriander
½ tsp ground allspice or garam masala
¼ of a whole nutmeg, finely grated
½ tsp ground turmeric
125g/5oz thick set natural yogurt
4 tbsps corn or vegetable oil
½ tsp chilli powder

1. Cut the chicken into 1-inch cubes. Sprinkle with ½ tsp salt from the specified amount, and the lemon juice – mix thoroughly, cover and keep aside for 30 minutes.

2. Put the rest of the ingredients into an electric food processor or liquidiser and blend until smooth.

3. Put this marinade into a sieve and hold the sieve over the chicken pieces. Press the marinade through the sieve with the back of a metal spoon until only a very coarse mixture is left.

4. Coat the chicken thoroughly with the sieved marinade, cover the container and leave to marinate for 6-8 hours or overnight in the refrigerator.

5. Preheat the oven to 230°C/450°F/Gas Mark 8.

6. Line a roasting tin with aluminium foil (this will help to maintain the high level of temperature required to cook the chicken quickly without drying it out).

7. Thread the chicken onto skewers, leaving ¼-inch gap between each piece (this is necessary for the heat to reach all sides of the chicken).

8. Place the skewers in the prepared roasting tin and brush with some of the remaining marinade.

9. Cook in the centre of the oven for 6-8 minutes.

10. Take the tin out of the oven, turn the skewers over and brush the pieces of chicken with the remaining marinade.

11. Return the tin to the oven and cook for a further 6-8 minutes.

12. Shake off any excess liquid from the chicken. (Strain the excess liquid and keep aside for Chicken Tikka Masala)

13. Place the skewers on a serving dish. You may take the tikka off the skewers if you wish, but allow the meat to cool slightly before removing from the skewers.

TIME Preparation takes 30-35 minutes plus time needed to marinate, cooking takes 15-18 minutes.

ONION BHAJIYAS

Onion Bhajiyas are popular all over India and have established themselves as a firm favourite in this country. They are made by coating finely shredded onions with a spicy batter.

SERVES 6-8

150g/6oz besan (gram or chick-pea flour)
1 tsp salt or to taste
Pinch of bicarbonate of soda
1 tbsp ground rice
2 tsps ground cumin
2 tsps ground coriander
½-1 tsp chilli powder
1-2 fresh green chillies, finely chopped and seeded if a milder flavour is preferred
2 large onions, sliced into half rings and separated
200ml/7fl oz water
Oil for deep frying

1. Sieve the besan and add the salt, bicarbonate of soda, ground rice, cumin, coriander, chilli powder and green chillies; mix well.

2. Now add the onions and mix thoroughly.

3. Gradually add the water and keep mixing until a soft but thick batter is formed and the onions are thoroughly coated with this batter.

4. Heat the oil over medium heat (*it is important to heat the oil to the correct temperature – 160-180° C*). To test this, take a tiny amount of the batter, about the size of a seed of a lemon and drop it in the oil. If it floats up to the surface immediately but without turning brown, the oil is at the correct temperature.

5. Using a tablespoon put in as many small amounts (about half a tablespoon) of the onion/batter mix as the pan will hold in a single layer. Take care not to make these amounts too large as this will result in the outside of the bhajiyas being overdone while the insides remain uncooked.

6. Reduce the heat to low as the bhajiyas need to be fried over a gentle heat to ensure that the batter at the centre of the bhajiyas is cooked, and stays soft, whilst the outside turns golden brown and crisp. This should take about 10-12 minutes for each batch.

7. Drain the bhajiyas on absorbent paper.

TIME Preparation takes 15-20 minutes, cooking takes 45-50 minutes.

SERVING IDEAS Serve on their own with drinks or with a selection of chutneys as a starter.
Suitable for freezing.

CHICKEN OR TURKEY PAKORAS

These delicious pakoras can be made with cooked as well as raw meat and it is therefore an excellent and unusual way to use left over Christmas turkey or Sunday roast. Raw chicken breast has been used for the recipe below, as they remain more succulent than cooked meat.

SERVES 6-8

150ml/5fl oz water

1 medium-size onion, coarsely chopped

2-3 cloves garlic, peeled and coarsely chopped

1-2 fresh green chillies, coarsely chopped; remove the seeds if you prefer a mild flavour

2 tbsps chopped coriander leaves

125g/5oz besan or gram flour/chick pea flour, sieved

1 tsp ground coriander

1 tsp ground cumin

½ tsp garam masala

½ tsp chilli powder

1 tsp salt or to taste

Pinch of bicarbonate of soda

325g/12oz fresh, boneless and skinless chicken or turkey breast

Oil for deep frying

1. Put 90ml/3fl oz water from the specified amount into an electric liquidiser followed by the onion, garlic, green chillies and coriander leaves. Blend until smooth. Alternatively, process the ingredients in a food processor without the water.

2. In a large bowl, mix the besan, coriander, cumin, garam masala, chilli powder, salt and bicarbonate of soda.

3. Add the liquidised ingredients and mix thoroughly.

4. Add the remaining water and mix well to form a thick paste.

5. Cut the chicken into pieces and gently mix into the paste until the pieces are fully coated.

6. Heat the oil over medium heat; when hot, using a tablespoon, put in one piece of besan-coated chicken/turkey at a time until you have as many as the pan will hold in a single layer without overcrowding it. Make sure that each piece is fully coated with the paste.

7. Adjust heat to low and fry the pakoras for 10-15 minutes turning them over half way through. Remove the pakoras with a perforated spoon and drain on absorbent paper.

TIME Preparation takes 20 minutes, cooking takes 30 minutes.

SERVING IDEAS Serve with Tomato Chutney or Green Coriander Chutney. Suitable for freezing.

POTATO PAKORAS

The Indian love of snacks is apparent in the wide range of mouthwatering recipes created to suit different occasions. These spice-coated crunchy potato slices are easy to make and can be served in a number of different ways.

SERVES 4-6

50g/2oz besan (gram flour or chick pea flour)
1 tbsp ground rice
½ tsp salt or to taste
1½ tsps ground coriander
1 tsp ground cumin
½ tsp chilli powder
50ml/2fl oz water
450g/1lb medium-sized potatoes, peeled and cut into ¼-inch thick slices
Oil for deep frying

1. Mix all the dry ingredients in a large bowl.

2. Add the water and mix to thick paste.

3. Add the potatoes and mix until the potato slices are fully coated with the paste.

4. Heat the oil over medium heat in a deep pan (you can use a deep fat fryer or a chip pan without the basket) and put in as many of the coated potato slices as the pan will hold in a single layer.

5. Fry the pakoras until golden brown (6-8 minutes).

6. Drain on absorbent paper.

TIME Preparation takes 10-15 minutes, cooking takes 20 minutes.

SERVING IDEAS Serve on their own with drinks; as a side dish with any meat, fish or chicken curry; or as a starter with Avocado Chutney.

VARIATION Use sweet potatoes.

WATCHPOINT Do not overcrowd the pan. This is to prevent the pakoras from sticking together.

MUSHROOM BHAJI

Although mushrooms are not widely used in India, the Indian restaurants in this country have popularised the use of mushrooms in Indian cookery. Mushroom Bhaji appears to be one of the most popular of them all.

SERVES 4

3-4 tbsps cooking oil
1 medium-sized onion, finely chopped
2-3 cloves garlic, peeled and crushed
½ tsp ground turmeric
½ tsp chilli powder
1 tsp ground coriander
1 tsp ground cumin
¾ tsp salt or to taste
1 tbsp tomato purée
225g/8oz mushrooms, chopped

1. Heat the oil over medium heat and fry the onions until they are lightly browned.

2. Lower heat and add the garlic, turmeric, chilli powder, coriander and cumin. Stir and fry the spices and add about 1 tbsp water to prevent the spices from sticking to the bottom of the pan. As soon as this water dries up, add a little more. Continue doing this until you have fried the spices for about 5 minutes.

3. Add the salt and tomato purée, mix well and add the mushrooms. Stir until the ingredients are thoroughly mixed.

4. Sprinkle about 2 tbsps water and cover the pan. Simmer for 10 minutes.

5. The finished dish should have a little amount of gravy, but it should not be runny. If it appears to be a little runny, take the lid off and let the liquid evaporate until the gravy is reasonably thick.

TIME Preparation takes 15 minutes, cooking takes 20 minutes.

13

SPICED POTATO BITES

In Indian cookery, potatoes are used very imaginatively. Here, boiled potatoes are cut into small pieces and sautéed until they are brown and then flavoured with a light sprinkling of spices.

SERVES 6-8

700g/1½lbs potatoes
4 tbsps cooking oil
½ tbsp salt or to taste
¼ tsp garam masala
½ tsp ground cumin
½ tsp ground coriander
¼ - ½ tsp chilli powder

1. Boil the potatoes in their jacket, cool thoroughly, peel and dice them into 1-inch cubes.

2. In a wide shallow pan, preferably non-stick or cast iron, heat the oil over medium heat. It is important to have the right pan otherwise the potatoes will stick.

3. Add the potatoes and spread them evenly around the pan. Brown the potatoes evenly, stirring them occasionally.

4. When the potatoes are brown, sprinkle over the salt, garam masala, cumin, coriander and the chilli powder. Stir gently and mix until the potatoes are fully coated with the spices. Remove from the heat.

TIME Preparation takes 30 minutes to boil the potatoes plus time to cool them, cooking takes 10-12 minutes.

SERVING IDEAS Serve on cocktail sticks with drinks.

WATCHPOINT The potatoes must be allowed to cool thoroughly. Hot or warm potatoes crumble easily and therefore cannot be cut into neat pieces.

VEGETABLE SAMOSAS

As the majority of the Indian population is vegetarian, it is no wonder that the original recipe for samosas is a vegetarian one.

MAKES 18 Samosas

450g/1lb potatoes
2 tbsps cooking oil
½ tsp black mustard seeds
1 tsp cumin seeds
2 dried red chillies, coarsely chopped
1 medium-sized onion, finely chopped
1-2 fresh green chillies, coarsely chopped
    and seeded if a milder flavour is
    preferred
½ tsp ground turmeric
1 tsp ground coriander
1 tsp ground cumin
1 tsp salt or to taste
1 tbsp chopped coriander leaves

1. Boil the potatoes in their jacket, allow to cool thoroughly, then peel and dice them.

2. Heat the oil and add mustard seeds. As soon as they start crackling, add the cumin seeds and red chillies, and then the onions and green chillies. Fry till the onions are soft. Add the turmeric, coriander and cumin.

3. Stir quickly and add the potatoes and the salt.

4. Reduce heat to low, stir and cook until the potatoes are thoroughly mixed with the spices.

5. Remove from the heat and stir in the coriander leaves. Cool thoroughly before filling the samosas. Make the samosas as instructed in the pastry recipe given for Meat Samosas.

TIME Preparation takes about 60 minutes and cooking takes about 60 minutes.

VARIATION Use 225g/8oz cauliflower and 225g/8oz potatoes. Blanch the cauliflower in boiling salted water, drain and cut into small pieces (almost the same size as diced potatoes).

FISH BHOONA

SERVES 4

700g/1½lbs steak or fillets of any white fish
6 tbsps cooking oil

*Mix the following 4 ingredients
in a small bowl*
1 tbsp plain flour
¼ tsp ground turmeric
¼ tsp chilli powder
¼ tsp salt

1 large onion, coarsely chopped
½-inch cube of root ginger, peeled and
    coarsely chopped
2-4 cloves garlic, peeled and coarsely
    chopped
½ tsp ground turmeric
¼ tsp chilli powder
1 tsp ground coriander
½ tsp garam masala
1 small tin of tomatoes
150ml/5fl oz warm water
100g/4oz frozen garden peas
1 tsp salt or to taste
1 tbsp chopped coriander leaves

1. Skin the fish, wash and dry thoroughly
on absorbent paper and cut the fish into
approximately 2.5 × 5cm/1 × 2-inch pieces.

2. Heat 2 tbsps oil from the specified
amount, in a large frying pan, preferably
non-stick or cast iron, over medium heat.

3. Lightly dust the fish, one piece at a time,
in the seasoned flour and place in the hot
oil. Put in as many pieces as the pan will
hold in a single layer without overcrowding
it and adjust heat to medium-high. Fry the
fish until all the pieces are evenly browned.
This has to be done quickly in fairly hot oil
so that the fish is thoroughly sealed. Fry all
the fish this way and drain on absorbent
paper.

4. Put the onion, ginger and garlic into a
liquidiser or food processor and blend until
smooth.

5. Heat the remaining oil over medium heat
in a wide, shallow pan. Add the onion
mixture and stir. When the mixture is
heated through turn heat down to low, stir
and fry for 3-4 minutes.

6. Add the turmeric, chilli, coriander and
garam masala and fry for 4-5 minutes,
stirring continuously. During this time, from
the tin of tomatoes, add 1 tbsp juice at a
time to prevent the spices from sticking to
the bottom of the pan.

7. Now add one tomato at a time, along
with any remaining juice, breaking the
tomato with the back of the spoon. Cook
until the tomato is well incorporated into
the rest of the ingredients. Use up the rest
of the tomatoes in the same way.

8. Add the water, peas and salt. Bring to the
boil and add the fish. Cover and simmer for
5 to 6 minutes.

9. Remove from heat and sprinkle the
coriander leaves on top.

TIME Preparation takes 15-20 minutes, cooking takes 30-35 minutes.

MASALA MACHCHI

Masala Machchi or spicy fish is made by marinating fish in lemon juice and spices. The lemon juice gives the fish a rather smooth and velvety texture.

SERVES 4

Juice of half a lemon

1 small onion, peeled and coarsely chopped

2-3 cloves garlic, peeled and coarsely chopped

1-inch cube of root ginger, peeled and coarsely chopped

1-2 fresh green chillies, chopped; seed the chillies if you like a milder flavour

3 tbsps chopped coriander leaves

1 tsp salt or to taste

450g/1lb fillet of any white fish

90ml/3fl oz oil for shallow frying

To coat the fish

3 tbsps plain flour

1 egg, beaten

¼ tsp salt

¼ tsp chilli powder

1. Put the lemon juice, onion, garlic, ginger, green chillies, coriander leaves and 1 tsp salt into an electric liquidiser and blend until smooth.

2. Wash the fish gently and pat dry with absorbent paper. If you are using frozen fish, defrost thoroughly and then dry as for fresh fish.

3. Cut the fish into 1½ × 1-inch pieces. Put a light coating of the spice paste on all sides of each piece of fish, cover the container and leave to marinate in a cool place for 2-3 hours, or overnight in the refrigerator.

4. Mix the flour with the salt and chilli powder. Dust each piece of fish lightly with this, then dip in the beaten egg. Shallow fry in a single layer over medium heat until brown on both sides (2-3 minutes on each side). Drain on absorbent paper. Alternatively, deep fry the fish until golden brown and drain on absorbent paper.

TIME Preparation takes 15-20 minutes, cooking takes 12-15 minutes.

PRAWN CHILLI MASALA

This is a delicate but richly flavoured dish. In India, only fresh and juicy king prawns will do, but standard peeled prawns can be used for this recipe.

SERVES 4

75g/3oz unsalted butter

6 green cardamoms, split open the top of each pod

1-inch cube of root ginger, peeled and finely grated

3-4 cloves garlic, peeled and crushed

1 tbsp ground coriander

½ tsp ground turmeric

450g/1lb fresh peeled prawns

125g/5oz thick set natural yogurt

90ml/3fl oz water

1 tsp sugar

1 tsp salt or to taste

25g/1oz ground almonds

4-6 whole fresh green chillies

100g/4oz finely chopped onions

2 fresh green chillies, seeded and minced

½ tsp garam masala

1 tbsp chopped coriander leaves

1. Melt 50g/2oz butter from the specified amount over gentle heat and add the whole cardamoms, fry for 30 seconds and add the ginger and garlic. Stir and cook for 1 minute, then add the ground coriander and turmeric. Stir and fry for 30 seconds.

2. Add the prawns, turn the heat up to medium and cook for 5-6 minutes, stirring frequently.

3. Beat the yogurt until smooth, gradually add the water and beat until well blended. Add this mixture to the prawns, stir in the sugar and the salt, cover the pan and simmer for 5-6 minutes.

4. Add the ground almonds and the whole green chillies and cook, uncovered, for 5 minutes.

5. Meanwhile, fry the onions in the remaining 25g/1oz butter until they are just soft, but not brown. Add the minced green chillies and the garam masala; stir and fry for a further 1-2 minutes. Stir this mixture into the prawns along with any butter left in the pan. Remove the pan from the heat.

6. Put the prawns in a serving dish and garnish with the coriander leaves.

TIME Preparation takes 15 minutes, cooking takes 20-25 minutes.

TO FREEZE Suitable for freezing if fresh prawns are used.

23

MIXED VEGETABLE CURRY

A variety of seasonal vegetables are cooked together in a gravy flavoured by a few ground spices, onions and tomatoes. Whole green chillies are added towards the end to enhance the flavour of the dish and also to retain their fresh green colour.

SERVES 4-6

4-5 tbsps cooking oil
1 large onion, finely chopped
½-inch cube of root ginger, peeled and
    finely sliced
1 tsp ground turmeric
1 tsp ground coriander
1 tsp ground cumin
1 tsp paprika
4 small ripe tomatoes, skinned and
    chopped or a small can of tomatoes with
    the juice
225g/8oz potatoes, peeled and diced
75g/3oz french beans or dwarf beans,
    sliced
100g/4oz carrots, scraped and sliced
75g/3oz garden peas, shelled weight
450ml/15fl oz warm water
2-4 whole fresh green chillies
1 tsp garam masala
1 tsp salt or to taste
1 tbsp chopped coriander leaves

1. Heat the oil over medium heat and fry the onions until they are lightly browned. (6-7 minutes).

2. Add the ginger and fry for 30 seconds.

3. Adjust heat to low and add the turmeric, coriander, cumin and paprika. Stir and mix well.

4. Add half the tomatoes and fry for 2 minutes, stirring continuously.

5. Add all the vegetables and the water. Stir and mix well. Bring to the boil, cover and simmer until vegetables are tender (15-20 minutes).

6. Add the remaining tomatoes and the green chillies. Cover and simmer for 5-6 minutes.

7. Add the garam masala and salt, mix well. Stir in half the coriander leaves and remove from heat.

8. Put the vegetable curry into a serving dish and sprinkle the remaining coriander leaves on top.

TIME Preparation takes 25-30 minutes, cooking takes 30 minutes.

TO FREEZE Suitable for freezing, but omit the potatoes. Add pre-boiled diced potatoes during reheating.

WATCHPOINT Frozen peas and beans may be used for convenience, but the cooking time should be adjusted accordingly. Cook the fresh vegetables first and follow cooking time for frozen vegetables as per instructions on packets.

CHICKEN CHAAT

Recipes do not have to be elaborate to be tasty, and Chicken Chaat is a perfect example. Cubes of chicken meat, stir-fried with a light coating of spices look impressive with a colourful salad and taste superb.

SERVES 4

700g/1½lbs chicken breast, skinned and boned
1 tsp salt or to taste
2-3 cloves garlic, peeled and coarsely chopped
2 tbsps cooking oil
1½ tsps ground coriander
¼ tsp ground turmeric
¼-½ tsp chilli powder
1½ tbsps lemon juice
2 tbsps finely chopped coriander leaves

1. Wash the chicken and dry on absorbent paper. Cut into 1-inch cubes.

2. Add the salt to the garlic and crush to a smooth pulp.

3. Heat the oil in a frying pan, preferably non-stick or cast iron, over medium heat.

4. Add the garlic and fry until it is lightly browned.

5. Add the chicken and fry for 6-7 minutes, stirring constantly.

6. Add the ground coriander, turmeric and chilli powder. Fry for 3-4 minutes, stirring frequently. Remove from heat and stir in the lemon juice and coriander leaves.

TIME Preparation takes 15 minutes, cooking takes 12-15 minutes.

SERVING IDEAS Serve as a starter garnished with crispy lettuce leaves, sliced cucumber, raw sliced onion and wedges of lemon or with a selection of chutneys. Chicken Chaat can also be served with drinks on cocktail sticks, hot or cold.
Suitable for freezing.

CHICKEN DO-PIAZA

A fairly easy dish to prepare in which more than the usual quantity of onions are used. The name itself suggests the quantity of onions required, Do means twice and Piaz means onion. The literal translation would, therefore, be 'chicken with twice the amount of onions'.

SERVES 4-6

1.4kg/2½lbs chicken joints, skin removed
1 large onion, coarsely chopped
1-inch cube of root ginger, peeled and
    coarsely chopped
3-4 cloves garlic, peeled and coarsely
    chopped
4 tbsps cooking oil
1 tsp ground turmeric
1 tsp ground coriander
1 tsp ground cumin
¼-½ tsp chilli powder
1 small tin of tomatoes
175ml/6fl oz warm water
2 cinnamon sticks, each 2-inches long;
    broken up
4 green cardamoms; split open the top of
    each pod
4 whole cloves
2 dried bay leaves, crumpled
1¼ tsp salt or to taste
2 level tbsps ghee or unsalted butter
1 large onion, finely sliced
1 tbsp chopped coriander leaves (optional)

1. Cut each chicken breast into 3 pieces. If you are using legs, separate leg from thigh.

Wash and dry on absorbent paper or a cloth.

2. Place the chopped onion, ginger and garlic into a liquidiser or food processor and liquidise to a smooth paste, add a little water, if necessary, to facilitate blade movement.

3. Heat the oil over medium heat and add the liquidised ingredients. Stir and fry for 4-5 minutes.

4. Add turmeric, coriander, cumin and chilli powder. Fry for 4-5 minutes stirring frequently. During this time, from the tin of tomatoes, add 1 tbsp juice at a time to prevent the spices from sticking to the pan. When you have used up all the tomato juice, add the chicken and fry it over medium-high heat until the chicken has changed colour.

5. Add the water, cinnamon, cardomom, cloves, bay leaves, salt and the whole tomatoes. Bring to the boil, cover and simmer until the chicken is tender and the gravy is fairly thick (about 25 minutes). Cook uncovered, if necessary, to thicken the gravy.

6. Heat the ghee or butter and fry the sliced onion for 5 minutes. Add the onions along with the ghee to the chicken. Remove from heat and stir in the coriander leaves.

TIME Preparation takes 15 minutes, cooking takes 45 minutes.

VARIATION Use lamb, but adjust cooking time.

TANDOORI CHICKEN MASALA

The word masala means a combination of spices. In this recipe the chicken is simmered gently in a smooth velvety sauce flavoured with saffron, ground cardamom and cinnamon.

SERVES 4-6

1kg/2.2lbs cooked Tandoori Chicken (see separate recipe)
50g/2oz ghee or unsalted butter
1 large onion, finely chopped
½-inch cube of root ginger, peeled and crushed
2 cloves garlic, peeled and crushed
1 tsp ground cardamom
1 tsp ground cinnamon
¼ tsp chilli powder
1 tsp salt or to taste
125g/5oz soured cream
225ml/8fl oz warm stock; (made up of the reserved cooking liquid and warm water)
4 level tbsps ground almonds
2 tbsps milk
½ tsp saffron strands
25g/1oz toasted flaked almonds

1. Heat the ghee or butter over low heat and fry the onions until they are just soft, but not brown.

2. Add the ginger and garlic and fry for two minutes, stirring constantly.

3. Add the cardamom, cinnamon, chilli powder and salt and fry for 1 minute, stirring constantly.

4. Beat the soured cream with a fork until smooth, add half the stock while still beating. Add this mixture to the onions and bring the liquid to a slow simmer.

5. Add the remaining stock, cover the pan and simmer for 10 minutes.

6. Sprinkle the ground almonds evenly, stir and mix well and remove the pan from heat.

7. Heat the milk and soak the saffron strands in it for 10-15 minutes.

8. Arrange the tandoori chicken in a wide shallow pan. Hold a sieve over the pan and pour the sauce into it. Press with the back of a metal spoon to extract as much of the spiced mixture as possible as the onion pulp is necessary to add to the thickness of the gravy. Alternatively, liquidise the mixture until smooth and then pour over the chicken.

9. Sprinkle the saffron milk and all the saffron strands evenly over the chicken.

10. Place the pan back over gentle heat and bring the liquid to the boiling point. Cover the pan and simmer for 10 minutes, turning the chicken once or twice.

11. Put the chicken in a serving dish and garnish with the toasted almonds.

TIME Preparation takes 25-30 minutes plus time needed for marinating, cooking takes 25-30 minutes for the chicken and 20-25 minutes for the sauce.

31

ROGAN JOSH

Rogan Josh finds its origin in Kashmir, the northern-most state in India. In the recipe below, more than the usual quantity of spices are used, but these are toned down by using a large quantity of tomatoes and a little double cream.

SERVES 4-6

3 tbsps ghee or unsalted butter
1kg/2.2lbs leg of lamb, without bones, cut into 1½-inch cubes
1 tbsp ground cumin
1 tbsp ground coriander
1 tsp ground turmeric
1 tsp chilli powder
1-inch cube of root ginger, peeled and grated
2-4 cloves garlic, peeled and crushed
225g-275g/8-10oz onions, finely sliced
400g/14oz tin of tomatoes, chopped or whole
1 tbsp tomato purée
125ml/4fl oz warm water
1¼ tsps salt or to taste
90ml/3fl oz double cream
2 tsps garam masala
2 tbsps chopped coriander leaves

1. Melt 2 tbsps ghee or butter, from the specified amount, over medium heat and fry the meat in 2-3 batches until it changes colour. Remove each batch with a slotted spoon and keep aside.

2. Lower heat to minimum and add the cumin, coriander, turmeric, chilli powder, ginger and garlic. Stir and fry for 30 seconds.

3. Adjust heat to medium and add the meat along with all the ghee and juice in the container. Stir and fry for 3-4 minutes and add the onions. Fry for 5-6 minutes stirring frequently.

4. Now add the tomatoes and tomato purée – stir and cook for 2-3 minutes.

5. Add the water and salt, bring to the boil, cover and simmer until the meat is tender (about 60 minutes).

6. Stir in the cream and remove from heat.

7. In a separate pan melt the remaining ghee over medium heat and add the garam masala, stir briskly and add to the meat.

8. Transfer a little meat gravy to the pan in which the garam masala was fried – stir thoroughly to ensure that any remaining garam masala and ghee mixture is fully incorporated into the gravy and add this to the meat. Mix well.

9. Stir in the coriander leaves.

TIME Preparation takes 20 minutes, cooking takes 1 hour 30 minutes.

TO FREEZE Freeze before adding cream, garam masala and coriander leaves. Defrost thoroughly before reheating. Bring to the boil, add the cream and remove from heat. Add garam masala and coriander leaves.

VARIATION Use braising steak, but increase cooking time.

MEAT VINDALOO

Vindaloo is made by marinating the meat in vinegar and spices. It is traditionally a hot curry, but the quantity of chillies can be adjusted to suit individual taste.

SERVES 4-6

Grind the following 5 ingredients in a coffee grinder

2 tbsps coriander seeds

1 tbsp cumin seeds

6-8 dried red chillies

1 tbsps mustard seeds

½ tsp fenugreek seeds

3-4 tbsps cider or white wine vinegar

1 tsp ground turmeric

1-inch cube of root ginger, peeled and finely grated

3-4 cloves garlic, peeled and crushed

1kg/2.2lbs shoulder of lamb or stewing steak

4 tbsps cooking oil

1 large onion, finely chopped

1-2 tsps chilli powder

1 tsp paprika

1¼ tsps salt or to taste

450ml/15fl oz warm water

2-3 medium-sized potatoes

1 tbsp chopped coriander leaves, (optional)

1. In a large bowl, make a thick paste out of the ground spices, by adding the vinegar.

2. Add the turmeric, ginger and garlic. Mix thoroughly.

3. Trim off excess fat from the meat and cut into 1-inch cubes.

4. Add the meat and mix it well so that all the pieces are fully coated with the paste. Cover the bowl with cling film and leave to marinate for 4-6 hours or overnight in the refrigerator.

5. Put the meat in a pan and place this over medium heat, allow the meat to heat through, stirring occasionally; this will take about 5 minutes. Cover the pan, and cook the meat in its own juice for 15-20 minutes or until the liquid is reduced to a thick paste. Stir occasionally during this time to ensure that the meat does not stick to the bottom of the pan. Remove from heat and keep aside.

6. Heat the oil over medium heat and fry the onions until they are soft (about 5 minutes).

7. Add the meat and fry for 6-8 minutes stirring frequently.

8. Add the chilli powder, paprika and salt. Stir and fry for a further 2-3 minutes.

9. Add the water, bring to the boil, cover and simmer for 40-45 minutes or until the meat is nearly tender (beef will take longer to cook, check water level and add more water if necessary).

10. Meanwhile, peel and wash the potatoes. Cut them into approximately 1½-inch cubes. Add this to the meat and bring to the boil again. Cover the pan and simmer until the potatoes are cooked (15-20 minutes).

11. Turn the vindaloo on to a serving dish and sprinkle the coriander leaves on top.

TIME Preparation takes 10-15 minutes plus time needed for marinating, cooking takes 1 hour 15 minutes.

ALOO GOSHT

A well-known north-Indian lamb curry with a distinctive flavour imparted by the ghee which is used to brown the potatoes before being added to the curry.

SERVES 4-6

1kg/2.2lbs leg or shoulder of lamb

1¼ tsps salt or to taste

1-inch cube of root ginger, peeled and coarsely chopped

3-4 cloves garlic, peeled and coarsely chopped

2 tbsps ghee or unsalted butter

450g/1lb medium-sized potatoes, peeled and cut into 1½-inch cubes

3 tbsps cooking oil

1 large onion, finely chopped

3-4 dried red chillies

2 cinnamon sticks, 2-inch long each, broken up

Make a paste of the following 5 spices by adding 3 tbsps water

1 tbsp ground coriander

1 tsp ground allspice

1 tsp paprika

1 tsp ground turmeric

¼-½ tsp chilli powder

1 tbsp tomato purée

2 black cardamoms, split open the top of each pod

4-6 whole cloves

450ml/15fl oz warm water

1 tbsp lemon juice

2 tbsps chopped coriander leaves

1. Trim off excess fat from the meat and cut it into 1½-inch cubes.

2. Add the salt to the ginger and garlic and crush to a pulp.

3. Melt the ghee or butter over medium heat in a non-stick or cast iron pan and fry the potatoes until they are well-browned on all sides (about 10 minutes). Remove the potatoes with a slotted spoon and keep aside.

4. Add the oil to any remaining ghee in the pan and when hot, fry the onions, red chillies and cinnamon sticks until the onions are soft (about 5 minutes).

5. Add the ginger and garlic pulp, and fry for a further 2-3 minutes stirring frequently.

6. Adjust heat to low and add the spice paste, stir and fry for 3-4 minutes.

7. Add the meat, adjust heat to medium-high, stir and fry until the meat changes colour (5-6 minutes), then stir in the tomato purée.

8. Now add the cardamoms, cloves and the water. Bring to the boil, cover and simmer for 45-50 minutes or 20 minutes in the pressure cooker with the 15lbs weight on.

9. Add the potatoes, bring to the boil again, cover and simmer for 15-20 minutes or until the potatoes are tender; if using pressure cooker, bring pressure down first, remove lid and add the potatoes. Cover and cook the potatoes without the weight.

10. Remove from heat and add the lemon juice and coriander leaves.

TIME Preparation takes 20-25 minutes, cooking takes 1 hour 30 minutes.

SHAHI KORMA

The word 'Shahi' means royal, so the title itself is evidence that this particular korma was created in the royal kitchens of the great Maharajas of India. The dish is rich and creamy and is a perfect choice for a special occasion.

SERVES 4-6

1kg/2.2lbs boned leg of lamb, fat trimmed and cut into 1½-inch cubes

125g/5oz thick set natural yogurt

½-inch cube of root ginger, peeled and grated

3-4 cloves of garlic, peeled and crushed

50g/2oz ghee or unsalted butter

2 medium-sized onions, finely chopped

Grind the following ingredients in a coffee grinder

2 tbsps coriander seeds

8 green cardamoms with the skin on

10 whole black peppercorns

3-4 dried red chillies

Mix the following 2 spices with the above ground ingredients

1 tsp ground cinnamon

1 tsp ground mace

3-4 tbsps chopped fresh mint or 1½ tsps dried or bottled mint

50g/2oz ground almonds

300ml/10fl oz warm water

½ tsp saffron strands, crushed

1½ tsp salt or to taste

50g/2oz raw split cashews

150ml/5fl oz single cream

1 tbsp rosewater

1. Put the meat into a bowl and add the yogurt, ginger and garlic. Mix thoroughly, cover the bowl with cling film and leave to marinate for 2-4 hours or overnight in the refrigerator.

2. Put the marinated meat, along with any remaining marinade in the container, in a heavy-based saucepan and place it over medium-low heat. Bring to a slow simmer, cover and cook the meat in its own juice for 45-50 minutes stirring occasionally. Remove the pan from the heat and lift the meat with a slotted spoon. Transfer the meat to another container and keep hot.

3. Melt the ghee over medium heat and fry the onions until they are lightly browned (8-9 minutes).

4. Adjust heat to low and add the ground ingredients and the mint; stir and fry for 2-3 minutes. Add the half of the liquid in which the meat was cooked, stir and cook for 1-2 minutes. Add the ground almonds and mix thoroughly; add the remaining meat stock, stir and cook for a further 1-2 minutes.

5. Adjust heat to medium and add the meat, stir and fry the meat for 5-6 minutes.

6. Add the water, saffron strands, salt and cashews, bring the liquid to a slow boil, cover and simmer for 20 minutes.

7. Add the cream, stir and mix well, simmer uncovered for 6-8 minutes.

8. Stir in the rosewater and remove from the heat.

TIME Preparation takes 20-25 minutes, cooking takes 1 hour 30 minutes.

MEAT MADRAS

This hot, but delicious curry is named after Madras, the major city in southern India, perhaps because in the humid south, people eat rather hot food. Strange though it may seem, this is because hot and spicy food makes one perspire, thereby cooling the body.

SERVES 4-6

6 tbsps cooking oil

2 medium-sized onions, coarsely chopped

1-inch cube of root ginger, peeled and coarsely chopped

3-4 cloves garlic, peeled and coarsely chopped

4-6 dried red chillies

2 large cloves garlic, peeled and crushed

1-2 fresh green chillies, sliced lengthwise

1 small tin of tomatoes

3 tsps ground cumin

1 tsp ground coriander

½-1 tsp chilli powder

1 tsp ground turmeric

1kg/2.2lbs leg or shoulder of lamb, fat removed and cut into 1½-inch cubes

175ml/6fl oz warm water

1¼ tsps salt or to taste

1 tsp garam masala

1. Heat 3 tbsps oil from the specified amount over medium heat and fry the onions, coarsely chopped ginger, garlic and red chillies until the onions are soft (8-10 minutes), stirring frequently. Remove from heat and allow to cool.

2. Meanwhile, heat the remaining oil over medium heat and fry the crushed garlic and green chillies until the garlic is lightly browned.

3. Add half the tomatoes, along with the juice; stir and cook for 1-2 minutes.

4. Add the cumin, coriander, chilli powder and turmeric, adjust heat to low and cook for 6-8 minutes, stirring frequently.

5. Add the meat and adjust heat to medium-high. Stir and fry until meat changes colour (5-6 minutes).

6. Add the water, bring to the boil, cover and simmer for 30 minutes.

7. Place the fried onion mixture in an electric blender or food processor and add the remaining tomatoes. Blend until smooth and add this to the meat – bring to the boil, add salt and mix well. Cover the pan and simmer for a further 35-40 minutes or until the meat is tender.

8. Stir in the garam masala and remove from heat.

TIME Preparation takes 25-30 minutes, cooking takes 1 hour 20 minutes.

WATCHPOINT Meat Madras is meant to be hot, but if you do not like it hot, omit the chilli powder and seed the green chillies.

PASANDA BADAM CURRY

Pasanda is a classic north Indian dish where the meat is cut into thin slices and cooked in a rich sauce containing saffron, yogurt and cream.

SERVES 4-6

900g/2lbs boned leg of lamb

1-inch cube of root ginger, peeled and coarsely chopped

4-6 cloves garlic, peeled and coarsely chopped

2 fresh green chillies, seeded and coarsely chopped

4 tbsps natural yogurt

50g/2oz ghee or unsalted butter

3 medium-sized onions, finely sliced

½ tsp ground turmeric

1 tsp ground cumin

2 tsps ground coriander

½ tsp ground nutmeg

¼-½ tsp chilli powder

225ml/8fl oz warm water

1¼ tsps salt or to taste

150ml/5fl oz single cream

25g/1oz ground almonds

1 tsp garam masala or ground mixed spice

2 tbsps rosewater

½ tsp paprika

---

1. Beat the meat with a meat mallet to flatten it to ¼-inch thickness, then cut into thin slices (about 1½-inch long and ½-inch wide).

2. Put the ginger, garlic, green chillies and yogurt into an electric liquidiser or food processor and blend until smooth.

3. Melt the ghee or butter over medium heat and fry the onions until they are lightly browned (6-8 minutes).

4. Add the turmeric, cumin, coriander, nutmeg and chilli powder; adjust heat to low, stir and fry for 2-3 minutes.

5. Add the meat and fry it over high heat for 3-4 minutes or until it changes colour.

6. Add about 2 tbsps of the liquidised ingredients and cook for 1-2 minutes, stirring frequently. Repeat this process until all the yogurt mixture is used up.

7. Now fry the meat over medium heat for 4-5 minutes stirring frequently. When the fat begins to seep through the thick spice paste and floats on the surface, add the water, bring to the boil, cover the pan and simmer until the meat is tender (about 60 minutes), stirring occasionally.

8. Add the salt, cream and ground almonds and let it simmer without the lid for 5-6 minutes.

9. Stir in the garam masala and rosewater and remove from heat.

10. Put the pasanda into a serving dish and sprinkle the paprika on top.

TIME Preparation takes 30 minutes, cooking takes 1 hour 20 minutes.

VARIATION Use braising steak.

Naan

Naan is traditionally cooked in the Tandoor. It is not difficult to cook naan in a very hot oven, although the distinctive taste of clay cooking will be missing.

MAKES 8 Naan

450g/1lb plain flour
1 tsp salt
1 tsp Kalonji-onion seeds, (optional)
1 tsp sugar
1½ sachets fast action or easy dissolve yeast
50ml/3fl oz milk
125g/5oz natural yogurt
1 medium-sized egg, beaten
50g/2oz ghee or butter
2 tbsps sesame seeds or white poppy seeds

1. Put the flour, salt, kalonji, sugar and yeast into a large bowl and mix well.

2. Warm the milk until it is lukewarm, reserve 1 tbsp yogurt and add the rest to the milk and blend thoroughly.

3. Beat the egg and keep aside.

4. Melt the butter or ghee.

5. Add the milk and yogurt mixture, egg and ghee or butter to the flour, knead with your hands or in the food processor or mixer until a soft and springy dough is formed.

6. Place the dough in a large plastic food bag and tie up the uppermost part so that the dough has enough room for expansion.

7. Rinse a bowl (preferably steel, as this will retain heat better) with hot water and put the bag of dough in it. Put the bowl in a warm place, until risen to double the original quantity (½-1 hour)

8. Divide the dough into 8 balls, cover them and keep aside for 10-15 minutes.

9. Preheat over to 230°C/450°F/Gas Mark 8 and put an ungreased baking sheet into the over to preheat for about 10 minutes. Remove baking sheet from the oven and line with a greased greaseproof paper or baking parchment.

10. Take one of the balls and stretch it gently with both hands to make a teardrop shape. Lay this on the baking sheet and press it gently to stretch it to about 6-7-inches in length, maintaining the teardrop shape at all times. Make 2-3 similar shapes at a time and brush with the reserved yogurt, then sprinkle with the sesame or poppy seeds. Bake on the top rung of the oven for 10-12 minutes, or until puffed and browned.

TIME Preparation takes 10-15 minutes plus time needed to prove the dough, cooking takes 20-25 minutes.

VARIATION Use 1 tsp caraway or cumin seeds instead of the onion seeds while making the dough.

CHAPATTIES

A Chapattie is a dry roasted unleavened bread best eaten as soon as it is cooked.
They are not as filling as Rotis or Parathas, so 2-3 chapatties per person
is quite normal.

MAKES 14 Chapatties

325g/12oz fine wholemeal flour or Atta/
  Chapatti flour
½ tsp salt
1 tbsp butter, or ghee
170ml-280ml/6-10fl oz warm water
  (quantity depends on the texture of the
  flour)
1 tbsp extra flour in a shallow bowl or plate

1. Food Mixer Method: Place the flour, salt and fat together in the bowl and mix thoroughly at the medium-to-low speed taking care to see that all the fat has been broken up and well incorporated into the flour. Turn speed down to minimum and gradually add the water. When the dough is formed, knead it until it is soft and pliable. Cover the dough with a well-moistened cloth and keep aside for ½-1 hour.

2. Hand Method: Put the flour and salt in a large bowl and rub in the fat. Gradually add the water and keep mixing and kneading until a soft and pliable dough is formed. Cover the dough as above and keep aside.

3. Divide the dough into 14 walnut-sized portions. Roll each portion in a circular motion between the palms to make a smooth round ball, then flatten the ball to make a round cake. Dip each cake into the dry flour and roll the chapatti into a disc of about 6-inch diameter.

4. An iron griddle is normally used for cooking chapattis, but if you do not have one, then make sure you use a heavy-based frying pan as the chapatties need even distribution of heat during cooking. Overheating of the pan will cause the chapatties to stick to the pan and burn.

5. Heat the griddle or frying pan over medium heat and place a chapatti on it, cook for 30 seconds and turn the chapatti over. Cook until brown spots appear on both sides, turning it over frequently.

6. To keep the chapatties warm, line a piece of aluminium foil with absorbent paper and place the chapatties on one end, cover with the other end and seal the edges.

TIME Preparation takes 20-25 minutes, cooking takes 35-40 minutes.

SERVING IDEAS Serve with any meat, chicken or vegetable curry
Suitable for freezing.

FRIED BROWN RICE

This is the traditional rice dish which accompanies chicken or meat dhansak. It can also be served with a host of other dishes.

SERVES 4-6

275g/10oz basmati or other long grain rice
4 tbsps cooking oil
4 tsps sugar
1 tsp cumin seeds
2 cinnamon sticks, 2-inches long each,
    broken up
6 whole cloves
6 black peppercorns
2 bay leaves, crumpled
570ml/20fl oz water
1 tsp salt

1. Wash the rice and soak in cold water for 30 minutes. Drain well.

2. In a heavy-based saucepan, heat the oil over medium heat and add the sugar.

3. The sugar will gradually begin to change colour to a dark brown. As soon as it does, add the cumin seeds, cinnamon, cloves, black peppercorns and bay leaves. Fry for 30 seconds.

4. Add the rice and fry for about 5 minutes, stirring frequently and lowering heat towards the last minute or two.

5. Add the water and salt. Bring to the boil, cover and simmer without lifting the lid: 12-15 minutes for basmati rice, 15-18 minutes for other long grain rice.

6. Remove the pan from heat and keep it undisturbed for a further 10-15 minutes before serving.

TIME Preparation takes a few minutes plus time needed to soak the rice, cooking takes 20-25 minutes.

WATCHPOINT If the lid is lifted and the rice is stirred during cooking, the loss of steam will cause the rice to stick and turn soggy. Do not handle the rice immediately after it has been cooked to ensure dry and separate grains.

PILAU RICE

Pilau is usually a beautifully fragrant rice or a combination of rice and meat, poultry, fish or vegetables. It is always cooked in pure butterfat ghee, but unsalted butter is a good substitute.

SERVES 4-6

275g/10oz basmati rice

50g/2oz ghee or unsalted butter

1 large onion, finely sliced

2-4 cloves garlic, peeled and finely chopped

8 whole cloves

8 green cardamoms, split open the top of each pod

2 cinnamon sticks, 2-inches long each, broken up

8 whole peppercorns

1 tsp ground turmeric

570ml/20fl oz water

1¼ tsps salt or to taste

1 heaped tsp butter

25g/1oz seedless sultanas

25g/1oz flaked almonds

1. Wash the rice and soak in cold water for ½ an hour. Drain well.

2. In a heavy-based pan melt the ghee or butter over medium heat and fry onions until they are soft but not brown (about 5 minutes).

3. Add the garlic, cloves, cardamoms, cinnamon sticks and peppercorns. Stir and fry until the onions are golden brown (3-4 minutes).

4. Add the rice and turmeric, stir and fry for 1-2 minutes. Adjust heat to low, stir and fry the rice for a further 2-3 minutes.

5. Add the water and the salt, bring to the boil, cover and simmer for 15 minutes without lifting the lid.

6. Remove the pan from heat and keep it undisturbed for a further 10-12 minutes.

7. Melt the 1 tsp butter over gentle heat and fry sultanas until they change colour and swell up (1 minute). Transfer the sultanas onto a plate and in the same fat fry the almonds until they are lightly browned. Remove and put onto a separate plate.

8. Put the pilau rice into a serving dish and, using a fork, gently mix in the fried sultanas and almonds.

TIME Preparation takes 10 minutes plus time needed to soak the rice, cooking takes 25-30 minutes.

VARIATION Omit the almonds and use a hard-boiled sliced egg to garnish.

CAULIFLOWER MASALA

This dish, with potatoes and peas, is flavoured with a few basic ingredients and the finished dish is semi-dry, making it an ideal accompaniment to rice and curry or Indian bread.

SERVES 4-6

1 medium-sized cauliflower
2 medium-sized potatoes
4 tbsps cooking oil
1 tsp cumin seeds
1 large onion
½ tsp ground turmeric
1 tsp ground coriander
1 tsp ground cumin
¼-½ tsp chilli powder
2 ripe tomatoes, skinned and chopped
175ml/6fl oz warm water
100g/4oz shelled peas, fresh or frozen
    (cook fresh peas until they are tender
    before using)
1-2 fresh green chillies, seeded and slit
    lengthwise into halves
1 tsp salt or to taste
½ tsp garam masala
1 tbsp chopped coriander leaves

1. Cut the cauliflower into ½-inch diameter florets – wash and drain.

2. Peel and cut the potatoes lengthwise into thick strips about ½-inch.

3. Heat the oil over medium heat and add the cumin seeds. As soon as they start popping, add the onions and fry until they are soft (about 5 minutes).

4. Turn heat down to low and add the turmeric, coriander, cumin and chilli powder. Stir and fry for 2-3 minutes and add the chopped tomatoes. Fry for a further 2-3 minutes stirring continuously.

5. Add the potatoes and the water. Bring to the boil, cover the pan and simmer until the potatoes are half-cooked.

6. Add the cauliflower, cover the pan again and simmer until the potatoes are tender (about 10 minutes).

7. Stir in the peas, green chillies, salt and garam masala. Cover and cook for 5 minutes.

8. Remove from heat and stir in the coriander leaves.

TIME Preparation takes about 25 minutes, cooking takes 30-35 minutes.

VARIATION Cook in 1½oz/45g ghee instead of oil for a richer flavour.

TARKA DHAL (SPICED LENTILS)

*Dhal of some sort is always cooked as part of a meal in an Indian household.
As a vast majority of the Indian population is vegetarian, dhal is a good
source of protein.*

SERVES 4

150g/6oz Masoor dhal (red split lentils)
750ml/1¼ pint water
1 tsp ground turmeric
1 tsp ground cumin
1 tsp salt or to taste
25g/1oz ghee or unsalted butter
1 medium-sized onion, finely chopped
2 cloves garlic, peeled and finely chopped
2 dried red chillies, coarsely chopped

1. Put the dhal, water, turmeric, cumin and
salt into a saucepan and bring the liquid to
the boil.

2. Reduce heat to medium and cook
uncovered for 8-10 minutes, stirring
frequently.

3. Now cover the pan and simmer for 30
minutes, stirring occasionally.

4. Remove the dhal from the heat, allow to
cool slightly and mash through a sieve.

5. Melt the ghee or butter over medium
heat and fry the onion, garlic and red
chillies until the onions are well browned
(8-10 minutes).

6. Stir in half the fried onion mixture to the
dhal and put the dhal in a serving dish.
Arrange the remaining fried onions on top.

TIME Preparation takes about 10 minutes, cooking takes about 50 minutes.

WATCHPOINT Pulses tend to froth and spill over. The initial cooking
without the lid in stage 2 should help to eliminate this problem, but should
you find that it is spilling over, then partially cover the pan until the froth
settles down; this should take only a few minutes.

Avocado Chutney

Avocado and cottage cheese are combined with a few selected fresh ingredients to make a mouthwatering dish.

SERVES 6-8

1 ripe avocado
Juice of half a lemon
50g/2oz plain cottage cheese
1 clove garlic, peeled and chopped
2 tbsps chopped coriander leaves
1 fresh green chilli, chopped and seeded if
    a milder flavour is preferred
½ tsp salt or to taste

1. Cut the avocado lengthwise into two and remove the stone. Scoop out the flesh.

2. Put the lemon juice in an electric blender or food processor and add the avocado along with the rest of the ingredients. Blend until smooth, add a little water if necessary, to facilitate blade movement in the blender.

TIME Preparation takes 5-10 minutes.

SERVING IDEAS Serve as a dip with Kababs, Samosas and Pakoras.

COCONUT STUFFED PANCAKES

Coconut is used for both sweet and savoury dishes in southern India. There is no substitute for freshly grated coconut, but as it is quite time consuming, desiccated coconut is a good compromise.

MAKES 6 pancakes

For the filling

50g/2oz desiccated coconut
50g/2oz soft dark brown sugar
25g/1oz walnut pieces, lightly crushed
1 small tin evaporated milk
1 tsp ground cardamom

1. Mix all ingredients, except ground cardamom, in a small saucepan and place over medium heat. As soon as it begins to bubble, reduce heat to low and let it simmer without a lid for 8-10 minutes stirring occasionally.

2. Stir in the ground cardamom, remove the pan from heat and allow the mixture to cool.

For the pancakes

2 eggs
150g/6oz wholemeal flour
1 tsp ground cinnamon
1 tbsp caster sugar
200ml/7fl oz milk
Ghee or unsalted butter for frying

1. Put all ingredients, except ghee or butter, in a large bowl and beat with a wire beater until smooth. This batter can also be prepared in a liquidiser or food processor.

2. Place a non-stick or cast iron frying pan over low heat, when hot, spread a little (about ¼ tsp) ghee or butter on it.

3. Pour about 2 tbsps of the batter in the pan and spread it quickly by tilting the pan. Pouring off the batter must be done quickly in one go to prevent it from setting before you have a chance to spread it. It is easier to measure each 2 tbsps into a cup or a small bowl before pouring into the pan.

4. In a minute or so, the pancake will set, let it cook for a further minute, then carefully turn it over with a thin spatula or toss it! Cook the other side for about 1 minute (brown spots should appear on both sides).

5. Spread 1 tbsp of the stuffing on one side of the pancake and roll it into a cylinder shape. Make the rest of the pancakes the same way.

TIME Preparation takes 15-20 minutes, cooking takes 50 minutes.

SERVING IDEAS Serve on their own as a tea-time snack or topped with a little whipped cream as a dessert.

WATCHPOINT Use a wide, thin spatula to turn the pancakes; wooden spatulas are too thick and they will squash the pancakes. Steel or plastic slotted spatulas are ideal.

SPICED MANGO FOOL

In India, mango is considered to be the king of all fruits. The taste of this tropical fruit, which grows extensively in India, is simply delicious.

SERVES 6-8

2 tbsps milk
¼ tsp saffron strands
170g/6oz evaporated milk
50g/2oz sugar
1 level tbsp fine semolina
2 heaped tbsps ground almonds
1 tsp ground cardamom
450g/1lb mango pulp or 2 × 425g/15oz tins
    of mangoes, drained and puréed
250g/9oz unflavoured fromage frais

1. Put the milk into a small saucepan and bring to the boil. Stir in the saffron strands, remove from the heat, cover the pan and keep aside.

2. Put the evaporated milk and sugar into a saucepan and place it over a low heat.

3. When it begins to bubble, sprinkle the semolina over, stir until well blended.

4. Now add the ground almonds, stir and cook until the mixture thickens (5-6 minutes).

5. Stir in the ground cardamom and remove from heat. Allow this to cool completely, then gradually beat in the mango pulp, making sure there are no lumps.

6. In a large mixing bowl beat the fromage frais with a fork, gradually beat in the evaporated milk and mango mixture.

7. Stir in the saffron milk along with all the strands as these will continue to impart their colour and flavour into the mango pulp. Mix well.

8. Put the mango pulp into a serving dish and chill for 2-3 hours.

TIME Preparation takes 10 minutes, cooking takes 10-15 minutes.

VARIATION Top the dessert with a few strawberries for an attractive look.

SPICED FRUIT SALAD

A novel deviation from traditional Indian desserts, but an excellent one to round off an Indian meal. Handle the tinned mango slices very carefully as they tend to be far too soft. Use fresh mangoes instead if you have a friendly bank manager!

SERVES 6-8

425g/15oz tin pineapple chunks
425g/15oz tin papaya (paw paw) chunks
425g/15oz tin mango slices, cut into chunks
425g/15oz tin guava halves, cut into chunks
3 cinnamon sticks, each 2-inches long
3 black cardamoms
6 whole cloves
8 black peppercorns

1. Drain all the fruits and reserve the syrup. Mix all the syrup together, reserve 570ml/20fl oz and drain off remainder.

2. Put the syrup into a saucepan and add the spices, bring to the boil, cover the pan and let it simmer for 20 minutes.

3. Uncover and reduce the syrup to half its original volume by boiling for 5-6 minutes. Remove from heat and allow the syrup to cool.

4. Keep the pan covered until the syrup cools, (in an open pan some of the flavour will be lost).

5. Reserve a few pieces of papaya and guava and all the mangoes. Arrange the remaining fruits in a serving bowl.

6. Arrange the mangoes on top, then put in the reserved papaya and guava.

7. Strain the spiced syrup and pour over the fruits. Cover with cling film and chill.

TIME Preparation takes 10-15 minutes, cooking takes 20 minutes.

VARIATION Use fresh ripe William pear instead of tinned mango.
Add 1 tbsp of brandy to the syrup.

INDEX